Castles in the Sky

by

W. Michael Armbruster

authorHOUSE™

1663 LIBERTY DRIVE, SUITE 200
BLOOMINGTON, INDIANA 47403
(800) 839-8640
WWW.AUTHORHOUSE.COM

First published by AuthorHouse 09/09/04

ISBN: 1-4184-0265-6 (sc)

Library of Congress Control Number: 2004093308

Printed in the United States of America
Bloomington, Indiana

This book is printed on acid-free paper.

This book is dedicated to

Jesus,
Family, Friends, and all those who
Let me learn,
Helped me learn,
Made me learn.

And of course,
This is dedicated to you.

Preface

The poems in this book were written not to publish but to express an emotion or feeling that was strong enough to move my fingers at the keyboard or the pencil in my hand. Most of the people who have affected me or caused me to write probably don't know who they are, but it is to those people I owe a great deal.

The persistence of my daughter Michelle in wishing to see what she calls 'my best poetry' in print has caused me to assemble again some of my poems into this book. Michelle, I hope you enjoy this collection and it meets your expectations.

I must also thank those who have encouraged me to write and share, especially my wonderful children Jason and Michelle, my parents, sisters and their husbands and children, who have given me so much love and understanding over the years. I have no doubt I have the best family in the world!

Hopefully, you can see that although the Dungeons may be dark and deep, the Corridors may be confusing at times, and the Courtyard is full of both good and bad things, there is a Light: not at the end of the tunnel but Above as well as With us all! I pray you May all see and feel that Light. It is waiting for you.

And now....

The Castle in the Sky

Castle: a large fortified building or group of buildings with thick, tall walls, usually dominating the countryside, surrounded by a protective barrier of water called a moat.

Courtyard: the open space in the midst of the castle surrounded by walls or buildings. Everyone gathers here, most social events take place here. Here is the very center of humanity, where relationships are begun, commerce takes place, and the day-to-day activities of life are lived.

Corridor: the pathways between the rooms and parts of the castle. Decisions you make in the corridor may cause you to ascend to the turret and be bathed in happiness or descend to the dungeon and be swallowed by sadness, or just exit into the courtyard to continue with the journey of life.

Dungeon: a dark, often underground, chamber or cell used to confine prisoners. The saddest, loneliest place in the castle. People sometimes disappear into the dungeon and never return. You can be lost, alone, sad, or full of despair in your dungeon or in theirs.

Chapel: a place within the castle set aside for worship. A sanctuary away from the daily chores and activities where you can commune alone or together with God.

Turret: a small tower or tower-shaped projection on a castle. The Turret is the highest part of the castle where you have the most beautiful and peaceful view of the world. This is the ultimate vantage point for enjoying the wonders of nature and the universe: the perfect setting for romance. When you are in love and the one you love is in love with you, your hearts float together to the highest turret where you are on top of the world!

A Castle in the Sky

a place to live where everything turns out okay: real happiness, real eternal love, real God.

A refuge within reality characterized by fulfilled dreams of love and togetherness. It is a place where Truth and a dedication to God and Family rule each day.

Happiness is eternal, not temporary.

Of course, you are the Good Knight or the Beautiful Princess who helps govern the realm with kindness, compassion, and equality for all.

It can exist for you.

Table of Contents

The Courtyard *1*

    to… 2

    always. 3

    you change me 4

    Welding 5

    take a deep breath 6

    Gail 7

    just as i get used to the thought 8

    You could see them together 9

    i write of endless love 10

    War's taken its toll 11

    i'll return 12

    * I will continue on* 13

    victory 14

    i used to think 15

    thanks 16

    To Sherry: the girl with the golden smile 17

    Monday night 18

    as we lay there 19

    The workshop* 20

    Your Music 21

    i worry 22

    You surprised me 23

    want you here 24

    you were there again 25

    you rested 26

    after 28

    defeat 29

    the real fear 30

    I thought 31

    the champion 32

The Corridors: Where? Which way? *33*

    *it's like a box * 34

    a date with destiny 35

the confrontation 36

i wish 38

sometimes.. 40

expectations. 41

responding 42

Its okay. I knew I didn't fit 43

which way do I go? 44

In a minute... 45

if your heart needs to speak 46

there is more 47

spaces beyond.. 48

The Hidden Chamber *49*

* The dreamer * 50

And still, Hope 51

the dream world.. 52

My Simple Fantasy...................................... 53

across the skies 54

opposites.. 55

like a dream 56

how long? 57

drifting to you... 58

Some People... 59

I'll take these four days 60

The Dungeon *61*

Avernus.. 62

maybe its just me.. 63

once in every hundred or so years.............. 64

overheard.. 66

if i could have been 67

gone 68

miss.. 69

The Lonely Boy... 70

how can six hours 71

chaos.. 72

he was a bright kid 73

The rain. 74
my future was gone 75
i began missing you. 76
No warning 77
I remember your eyes 78
near death 79

The Chapel *80*
God 81
It was a beautiful day, Lord 82
slow me down, Lord 83
A Prayer for a Girl far away 84
She needs You, Lord 85
A Prayer 86
Teach me Lord 87
I, II, III 88

The Highest Turret: On Top of the World *89*
you are 90
touching you 91
just us 92
your kiss 93
i wish i knew what you're dreaming 94
holding hands 95
this I know. 96
even though 98
summer's song 99
Thank You For You 100
A song for you 101
there are so many things 102
they probably thought i was crazy 103
Addi 104
Angels 105
We will dance forever 106
until we met 107

The Courtyard

The Courtyard

to...

…to think
to dream
to have expectations
to believe in something.

…to see
to hear
to understand
to realize the truth.

…to cry
to feel foolish
to accept reality
to see life as it is.

…to be amazed
to be surprised
to be impressed
to be overwhelmed.

…to feel different
to undergo change
to discover a special world
to discard the old restricted dreams.

…to get lost in someone's eyes
to touch lips that melt your heart
to dissolve in the warmth of another's body
to feel happiness, and love, and happiness, and love …

…to live …

always.

always
  believing in you,
    having been delighted by your intelligence.

always
  hoping that you
    will finally find those solutions within.

always
  praying for your courage
    to act for what is right, what you deserve.

always
  sending you my strength
    to help you meet the challenges head on.

always
  wishing you smiles,
    happiness, laughter, and joy for the future.

always,

always
  sending you love
    from the depths of my heart to yours.

always.

you change me

tears

sadness

disappointment

swelling deep inside my chest..
the pressure, the shortness of breath..
it pulls me over, my shoulders sag with the weight..

sometimes it just seems like too much.

but then I feel the warmth of your heart
the goodness in your soul
and I am

strength

patience

focus.

Welding

welding
two girders of
solid, premolded steel
is not an easy task.

often weathered and tempered
by exposure to the elements
it becomes most difficult
to set the bond
so it will last.

sometimes
the heat needed
reaches such incredible
temperatures
that it's almost certain
both ingots will crack.

but with patience and care
each girder will give –
melting into the other
with the bond serving
as an unbreakable seal
to conquer the trials of time
and set a straight and true track.

take a deep breath

take a deep breath.

let it out slowly.

let the disappointment go with it.

    and the confusion.

        and the pain.

           and the urge to cry.

take a very, very, very deep breath.

let it out slowly.

now, go on.

Gail

Every young girl deserves a chance
To touch the top - to be the best,
But some, it seems, are left behind
Without a hope to pass the test.
    Since You decide who will pass or fail,
    I'm asking You, Lord, what about Gail?

Why should evil that others cause
Determine what another life will hold -
Why should mistakes that others make
Leave innocent girls hopeless - lost and cold?
    Is my pleading, Lord, of no avail?
    Can't You see, Lord, that I'm worried about Gail?

In the intertwined fates that guide us all
Through every hour and every day
Is there no way to cut the ropes
That keep the young from creating new ways?
    Can You hear, Lord, as my worries toss and sail
    My concern for that wonderful blonde girl, Gail?

She is trapped there in lower America
Where sex and money have a reach so broad
She has little chance for a decent life
Or to hide from those false, immoral gods.
    You can change it, Lord, you can change this tale:
    Please, Lord, will You give but one chance to Gail?

No one is free to help themselves
As long as they're alone in ghettos of dirt.
Without You God to give them hope
It's hard to be spared corruption's deep hurt.
    Only You vanquish evil, & help the young, innocent, & frail,
    So I'm praying to you, Lord, <u>please</u> help that girl Gail!

just as i get used to the thought

Just as i think i am getting used to the thought
that you are gone: that you are no longer here
the world again reminds me in some subtle way
of the person i love, so special and dear.

The woman sitting in the car next to me
has curly hair that looks soft, silky and dark
just like yours on that warm afternoon when we lay
together talking in that sunny green park.

Overhead the mid-day clouds have all disappeared
to expose a sky that is clear and very bright blue
taking my mind racing back to the beautiful day
we spent white water rafting – me rowing with you.

The piercing brown eyes of the woman i pass,
then a distinctive voice that might also be you,
yet again make me think of our time together
and the wonderful things you say and you do.

Even as the day closes and my weary head
lies alone on the pillow in the too quiet room
the silence itself speaks of the distance between us
growing greater, and i'm swallowed again by gloom.

As the night travels on, i finally succumb
to the memories that i know will fill my night
my last breath is a prayer that wherever you are
you are happy and safe, and your life is all right.

You could see them together

You could see them together, walking close, side-by-side
peering intently into each huge picture window,
admiring the wares that were offered there,
slowly investigating each individual shop.

Every now and then wandering closer,
Rubbing arms, shoulders, even hips,
her hand unconsciously reaching
to his elbow, sliding softly down
the familiar arm to rest securely
in the warm grasp of his hand.

They moved together as one,
Each in turn talking, then
listening to the other,
Discussing
the many items they saw,
the other people they had met,
everything from today's weather to
the state of peace throughout the world.

Her gentle smile as she softly spoke to him
echoed many, many years of contented happiness
As did the tender look emanating from his wise eyes
Each time they rested upon her for even a split second.

love.

i write of endless love

i write of endless loves
that only the poets have imagined;
of eternities of joy
transmitted through smiles and laughter.

i write of suffocating sorrow
so engulfing that death becomes freedom;
of hurt and failure and pain
transferred from your eyes to mine

i have journeyed afar without leaving my birthplace behind:
i have seen the grandeur of the Coliseum,
the white-capped peaks of Siberia.
i have felt the ocean's spray off Manila,
the relentless sun of the Sahara
i have seen lifetimes of dreams come true and have felt
happiness beyond compare

and i've done it
riding behind your eyes - a silent teardrop;
listening within your ears – a thief of memories;
feeling the beating of your heart – sharing its rhythm.

you have taught me shared with me ignored me hurt me loved me
unknowing you have given me a life where i sadly recount
sorrow, hurt, failure, and pain
yet i can joyously celebrate
timeless loves and endless happiness

and i thank you.

War's taken its toll

War's taken its toll of the human race,
We're still expanding and using up space,
Who knows what trials tomorrow we'll face,
But can't anybody face up to God?

To get ahead they now teach you to cheat
So you can trample the losers under your feet.
Then you can buy more affluence and never get beat,
But you haven't beaten my God!

To rebel is the thing – and if you are not 'in'
There's almost no chance that power you'll win.
You've got to conform before you begin,
But is anyone conforming to God?

False prophets around us preach their faith
As we're caught up between pollution and waste.
We spin with confusion as we dig our own grave –
But the spinning can end with God!!

i'll return

standing there in your
        pretty blue robe
        waving goodbye
you looked like a
        goddess; an angel
        from somewhere high in the sky.

i wanted to stop the car,
        turn around,
        and run back to you
to hold you close again
        and gaze into
        those eyes so blue.

but as always, fate
        was once more
        calling my name
so i had to leave
        and go alone
        in the falling rain.

if you save that smile
        for me, i'll return
        someday
and then maybe,
        next time,
        i'll be able to stay.

I will continue on

The October clouds drift lazily by,
As though they are watching, waiting
For someone to reach out and touch them.
They are headed the way the wind blows,
And are guided solely by chance
To their destinies.

I am not unlike a cloud.
Watching, Waiting for someone
To reach out to me; And knowing
That if you let me drift past,
I will continue onward, led by chance,
To another destiny.

victory

This is a day
For Victory

Today is the day
We must win

Anyone can win
On a clear sunlit
Afternoon
With all the elements
In perfect
Harmony

It is winning
On the cold snowy
Days enshrouded
By frozen winds
And heartless
Blizzards
That makes us grow

This is a day
For Victory

Today is a day
I will win.

i used to think

i used to think that nothing could compare
　　　　with the overwhelming glory of a summer sunrise.

　　　　life springs forth
　　　　as God's eyes open on the world
　　　　thriving on love, freedom, and
　　　　nature's sweet melodies.

i rode the sunrise
　　　　believing that the night would never come.

...now i've believed in too many sunrises,
i've cried in the dark of too many nights.
seen too many summers end
to believe in this sunrise.

Still, i would
　　　　like you to fly with me for a while
　　　　to spread our wings and soar,
　　　　let the breezes carry us
　　　　up, away, to the peace of the open sky.

together, perhaps, we can fly fast enough to beat the sunset.

thanks

This may sound kind of funny,
You may think I'm a little mad.
But thanks for helping my world be sunny
And for those moments together we had.

Just talking to a girl as fine as you
Makes my world seem a little more bright.
You're a wonderful girl, and beautiful too,
And I thank you for your time last night.

Money can buy a guy a lot of things
That you can play with, or look at, or hold,
But friendship is worth more than diamond rings
And is beyond the reach of silver and gold.

So thanks for the friendship and the time you spent
Just talking (and dancing) with me.
You'll never know how much those moments meant
Or how happy you helped me to be.

Thanks.

To Sherry: the girl with the golden smile

To Sherry: the girl with the golden smile
I send forth vibrations from my heart.
They thank you for talking to me awhile
When pangs of loneliness had begun to start.

When a boy loves a girl who's far away
Then minutes alone become hours of pain
And he needs a soft voice to brighten his day
To help him stand up and face life again.

I was alone - feeling empty and down
Then you filled me with an unexplainable joy
When you smiled and softly asked me to sit down
When we talked - you and me - a girl and a boy.

I thank you for these joyous moments too few;
For those brief hours of friendship we had.
I hope your future holds happy days for you,
And that you'll always smile and never be sad.

Monday night

I went out tonight with the guys.
   (i'd really rather be with you).
In the midst of the fun i realized
   my heart was feeling kinda blue.

We sat and talked about the world
   but you were in my thoughts.
Insults were thrown and indignities hurled
   (aimed at you they were not.)

The voices grew louder, the sound increased
   until the car was filled with noise.
Still, in my ear all vibrations ceased
   for my thoughts were far from 'the boys'.

Where you are tonight i do not know:
   i hope you're having lots of fun.
I pray when you leave, wherever you go,
   that your life is filled with shining sun.

I'm sort of afraid of what may transpire
   when you are so far out of my sight.
My whole life would become a funeral pyre
   if something happened to you tonight.

"Why worry?" they say, "What can you do?"
   I can pray to the heavens above;
I can believe that once again i'll join you
   my light, my life, my love.

as we lay there

you spoke softly
as we lay there together,
your head on my chest, my arms around your shoulders.

you echoed those things I already knew, had fought, had lost to,
and had already accepted as a future I could not prevent.

I knew someday my dreams would need to be put away,
carefully folded into that toy box with my other childish ideas.

I knew when we met you could make me put them where they belong
but I didn't realize the happiness that would accompany the pain.

you spoke quietly again
voicing the tears that had tugged at my heart
ever since I realized the marvel and the person that you are.

you spoke yet again
I had to take a long, deep breath and hug you tightly
to force tears and dreams into the correct box, and slam the lid.

I know I was selfish when I wanted to give you and you to give me
the dreams of love I had carried since I was young.

I knew you could not because you are already a fantasy of your own,
an emissary of compassion I could not, did not want to change.

you looked at me with eyes of happiness, yet filled with a sadness
knowing the future was not what I, nor you, had planned.

you whispered to me again,
then turned to sleep: turning your back on me and my dreams,
and I let go of them, and they drifted off into the dark, lonely night.

The workshop*

The workbench was beaten and worn,
the old tools no longer fit,
the projects were all finished
and lay in the corner
where quiet memories sit.

I turned and I waved goodbye
to the workshop where I had lived,
to the wrinkled plans and drawings,
to the years and tears
I could no longer give.

The light of the many people,
those who helped me travel the miles
still conquered the hovering darkness,
sending me forth with their
songs and their smiles.

Behind, the open door beckoned me through
Never to return to the past.
I'd given the years all I could,
Now I began a new journey
with a strength that will last.

So I turned again, I faced today,
with open arms and eager mind
and reached to unlock the future
with ever growing excitement
at what we may discover or find.

I didn't look back when I stepped out,
I don't remember when I closed the door.
For the joy of the world
and the warmth of your smile
Has convinced me the workshop is there no more.

Your Music

We listened.
I learned.

Suddenly my chest tightened - it was bursting
With an enormous pressure from deep within -
An overwhelming, overpowering onslaught of pain
Shook my being from where I thought my heart had been.

The Disillusionment - the disappointment
That heart-rending pain that's held you in its grasp:
I felt darkness . . . loneliness . . . sorrow . . .
An encompassing sadness that crushed you in the past.

We listened
I learned.

Like magic the wall appeared and surrounded you
To keep your history hidden - keep it from repeating itself
Now independent - now self sufficient and self contained,
Now able to be strong and to live by yourself.

You know it's too hard to really trust now.
You'd have to unlock and open your fortress's gate,
And who really knows just when to slam it tight
Before you get hurt - before it's too late!

We listened
I learned.

That mood - the weather - raging within - changed
From the stormy battering of the not-so-far past
To a calmer, deeper, remote hidden place,
Perhaps where you found your safe refuge at last.

I felt your heart beat - I felt it swell
With the rising crescendos of the orchestras tide,
Your silence - your eyes - your body whispered
About unspoken dreams still hidden deep inside.

We listened.
I learned.

21

i worry

i worry
because you're so young
and haven't been out there yet
to learn to mistrust the world the way i do.

i worry
because you're so special
and I want for you to keep
being special - and unique - as you grow up.

i worry
because you're so good
and I've seen that goodness become a target
for the bad and the ugly in society.

i worry
for me too
because I'd be so alone and lost
if you weren't here to be my daughter and friend.

i worry
like every other father
wondering if i've given you the tools
to build a quality life when you go on your own.....

i worry
most of all
about if you and our God in heaven
can talk - and work things out - like we did before.....

<u>You surprised me</u>

You surprised me: I wasn't looking for you.

You made me laugh
at your quick wit and spontaneous humor,

you made me wonder
at your honesty and candor,

you made me marvel
at the way you make me feel.

You surprised me.

You made me comfortable
to be myself when i'm with you,

you made me relax
in your warm embrace,

you made me dream again
when your lips met mine.

You surprised me.

Your understanding
of my family and their needs,

your easy willingness
to pitch in and help with dinner,

your bold confrontations
when i challenge your independence.

You surprised me. I wasn't looking for you.

want you here

i want you here.

i want to see you in the morning
       to brush the sleep from your eyes
       to run my fingers through your tangled hair
       to give you a hug to let you know you can
            depend on me today.

i want to hold you in the morning
       before the makeup covers your natural beauty
       before the noise of traffic shatters our peace
       before the stresses of life flood back
            from our memories.

i want you here.

i want to hear the song of your voice start my day
       to see your smile challenge the sun's brightness
       to meet your eyes and see the clear understanding
       to know that you know you are
            surrounded by love.

i want to kiss you in the morning
       before your lips speak of the challenges of life
       before reality takes you from my castle
       before i have to share you with
            the world.

i want you here.

you were there again

You were sitting there
    across the crowded restaurant
        engaged in intense conversation
            that i know stopped for a second

When you saw me
    and took a quick glance
        at who i was with
            after all this time had passed

Because my heart also
    skipped a beat when i saw you
        and i looked to see who you were
            with after so very very long.

I know you wanted to
    cross the room and say 'hi'
        to try to take three quick minutes
            to fill in the missing years

Because i know you
    like i know me and i wanted
        to find out what life had given you
            hoping you would say happiness.

I know you are wondering now
    the same way i am wondering
        why we both just stayed in our seats
            not getting together after all. Again.

you rested

you quietly rested.

your red, weathered slats relaxed,
the paint was beginning to show
the ancient wood underneath.

the portals to the world
and from the world
were covered with boards
so no one could disturb
the past snuggled within your walls
hiding the single room inside,
the old desks no longer needed,
the worn out chalk board where
a thousand children accomplished
the goals of reading, addition,
the basics of biology.

you rested in silence now,
and the small bell
perched upon your weary roof
silently tolled memories
of laughing children,
of poems and lessons recited
by children of all ages,
of dreams and ambitions that
began within these walls,
of caring souls who took the time
to teach those who sought
more than they knew before,
of the happiness of learning,
of the sadness of moving on,
of the excitement of the future…

you rested,

radiating your years of learning,
proudly surveying your mountain valley,
watching the world continue,
knowing that it began here,
that you nurtured some souls,
        you planted some seeds,
        you began some dreams.

you rested,

satisfied,

knowing

you truly made a difference.

after

after
when you look back at us,
  I know you will think of the Magic
    that others saw surrounded us
      even before you and I would admit it was there.

after
I know my family will think
  of my telling them about you
    and of the happiness they knew I felt
      like none they'd ever seen before.

after
if my friends talk about me
  you will be in the conversation too
    since you were the one who brightened my life
      with an eternal sunshine that never saw the night.

after
there will never be any regrets,
  never any question about you and me
    anywhere in the depths of my mind,
      never any doubts about that Wonderful Magic.

after
when I kneel in front of God
  awaiting the Final Judgment
    I will still be thanking Him for you
      and the part of your life He let me share.

after.

defeat

after a defeat
the longest walk for an athlete
is the walk back.

after you lose
when you wanted, expected more
the walk is miles and miles.

after the final gun sounds
and you are not the victorious one
the road stretches on and on.

when its over
the fatigue, the disappointment, sets in
as the trip back begins.

especially
if you feel you could have done better
on the road in
particularly
if the preparation wasn't good enough
before you arrived.

sadly
if you feel partially responsible
for the loss

most of all,
the road back seems to stretch forever

when you are alone.

the real fear

the real fear is
knowing
I love you
knowing
I need you
knowing
I want you
knowing
you excite me
knowing
you thrill me
knowing
you make me smile
knowing
you make me happy
knowing
I make you smile
knowing
I make you happy

yet
not knowing
your heart

I thought

I thought us loving and sharing and hugging and holding
and caring and wanting and needing and talking and
communicating and happy times and sad times and
my experience and your experience and our experiences
together and your love my love and our
love…

Your compassion and your tears and my caring and my
tears and your smiles and my smiles and your laughter
and my laughter and our laughter together and your
background and my background and your knowledge
and my knowledge and the way we compliment each
other and your memory and my craziness and the way
the music so often was written for just us and then it
was played just at the right time for us and the way I
exaggerated and the way you were so exact and the
Magic…

God and honesty and truth and prayers together and
church and more love and your family and what you
are and my family and what I am and we were happy
together and yet I could help you be happier than you
had ever been and you would be even happier and you
could help me be even happier than I had ever been
and then I would be even happier and we worked and
played well as a team and so we could work as a team
in the world and try to help others in the world be happy
together too

But

I guess that It was not Enough and
I
thought
w
r
o
n
g
.

the champion

there I am in the arena,
competing with my team,
giving it my all, our all,
struggling against the odds,
straining to win the event.

I glance into the stands
and I see you sitting there
watching, cheering for me,
giving me support
as the game continues.

your presence inspires me,
helps me draw the best
from deep down inside,
and I become possessed with
a champion's ability
and our team plays likes it is on fire…
we score,
then score again,
and emerge the conquerors,
victorious.

Then reality sets in,
the dream world vanishes
and I see the empty places
in the stands
where you have never been,
where I have no reason to believe
you will ever be,
and the game goes on.

The Corridors: Where? Which way?

The Corridors...

Where?

Which Way?

*it's like a box *

It's like a box.
A toy box.

Being shaken around
with all the pieces
tumbling and whirling about.

only all the other toys
settle into their slots
or their special places.

All except me.

I continue to whirl
and flounder
and tumble
and fall

and I wonder

why?

a date with destiny

I have a date with destiny.

Not as far away as before. I know it now, I knew it then.
It was light-years away.

Now, six months have passed, and it draws closer.

But I don't know it's face yet, so I'm not sure how to prepare.

A parachute or a new red mustang?
Savings bonds or sandy beaches?

Life insurance and spring flings?
Lifting weights or lifting beers?

And will it be wearing....

> White.
> Or
> Pink
> or
> blue
> or
> Black.

I know the date is coming.

I know the options.

I know how to play the games.

I'm just not sure yet

which game.

the confrontation

I couldn't focus. Somehow, you had broken the unbreakable wall.
I knew it before, but today, today the fear overwhelmed me.

An urge, oh so great, seized my being.
Another warning.
"Return, Return, Return
To the comfortable, the known, the safe way."

Your eyes, so beautifully brown, so soft and loving, met mine
in the silence.

A friendly, familiar sound from the past began
a melody within my head, echoing within my heart,
calling to my very soul.   *"Fly."*

The confusion, the chaos swirled around me, around us.
"Turn", the voice sang softly, *"turn away."*
"Look to the sun!"
"Reach to the stars!"
"Find the open spaces, with fresh air you can breathe!"
"No one can control you out there, no one can stop you!"

Your hands touched mine.
"Remember." The soothing voice smoothly rolled across the
seconds.   *"Remember."*
"No boundaries. No fences. No pain."
"Places to go. Things to do. Projects. Purposes. People."

"Fly."

"Feel the wind against your face, at your back."
"Leave it all behind."

You lips touched mine.

"Soar into the sky."

The voice grew more insistent, more hurried.
The beat of the rhythm accelerated, the volume
of the song increased...

"Spread your wings before it is too late!"
"Jump!
Fly now!   Fly now!   Fly now!"

"Fly now!"

too late too late too late too late too late too late too late too late

Love.

i wish

i wish i could take this hurt from you
and replace it with the dreams,
the ideas, the fantasies that
you so much deserve, that
you should have been
given before and the
love you deserve
that you have
given and
should
get.

i wish for another time, another
day when you will be happy
with the smiles radiating
from your eyes and the
dimples decorating
your cheeks and
the laughter
flowing
again.

i wish that right now my God would
talk to you and let you know just
how very special you are to His
world and help you see the
difference you have
made in so very
many lives.

i wish that you could see
yourself just exactly
as those of us who
love you see you.
i wish you
would be
happy.

i wish you
love.

sometimes

Sometimes
being an anachronism
is harder than at other times…
Sometimes
the lack of a home
makes the wanderer wonder…

Sometimes
the drifting asteroid
looks longingly at the moon…
Sometimes
the baying lone wolf
wishes he were a dog…

Sometimes
the running river
longs to be a lake…
Sometimes
the mighty meteor
envies the meteorite…

Sometimes
the powerless
give in to the pressure…
Sometimes
the majestic mountain
crumbles and washes away…

Sometimes
it becomes evident
that there is no resting place…
Sometimes
It's so very hard
To see the Light at the end…

expectations.

expectations are a lot like dreams.

sometimes i think
        they are both pointless.

having them
        sets yourself or others
                up for disappointment
                    or failure
        and both can happen
                every day
                    and any day.

without them
        you just prepare yourself
                and take life as it comes
        and be happy
                with what you get.

expectations really are a lot like dreams.

responding

Lightning thundered across the darkened skies
of the dream world that engulfed me
shattering the shell in which I slept
as your cries resounded in the night.

Though the call was not for me,
I responded quickly,
as the Love for you within me
required, demanded.

When you were comforted,
and those demons that
haunted your dream world
were gone,
you slept...
I returned to where my dreams
awaited me.

Staring into the blackness,
I now could not longer sleep,
and as I prayed
that the dream worlds sanctuary
would overcome my being,
I realized that
in the joy of comforting you
I had found an emptiness
and I wondered
if
anyone would ever call
my name
in the night.

Its okay. I knew I didn't fit

Its okay. I knew I didn't fit.

You wanted me to become
       What your parents had produced
But instead I had my own plans and dreams
       that, I know, confounded and confused.

but it's okay. I understand your plan.

I created deep within my mind
       My own world of heroes and of sci-fi
Where brave men saved the princesses
       Where happy endings thrived and no one died.

yes, it's okay. I knew where I belonged.

the groups that formed within each school
       did not include a dreamer's slot.
with the athletes, rebels, and other types
       I was there dreaming of other plots..

its okay. I made my place anyway.

after many years ,she found my realm
       for a moment she stood right beside me
and opened up my eyes to all the world
       as well as my heart, so I could see.

Its okay, this place.

now what is left is not just pretend
       me living inside my own fantasy
God willing I will continue on for a while
       flying higher and faster, the Son shining on me.

really. relax. it is okay.

which way do I go?

Which way do I go now?

Back. To the Safe Place?

> All the Boxes neatly stacked with lids nailed on tight.
> Only a single mission. No feeling. No pain.

Out. To the Promise?

> All the Boxes neatly stacked with lids nailed on tight.
> Many goals. Much to do. Too busy for pain.

Away. To the Other?

> All the Boxes neatly stacked with lids nailed on tight.
> No goals. Not much to do but prepare.

Ahead. To You?

> All the Boxes open, their contents understood.
> A dream. A Fantasy. An illusion. Love.

????

In a minute

In a minute,
I said.

In a minute,
I'll probably get the message
I'll probably realize the answer
I'll probably finally have a clue.

In a minute,
I'll probably have an awakening
I'll probably undergo a transformation
I'll probably understand your words.

In a minute,
I'll probably be aware of what's happening
I'll probably realize reality will
probably dismiss my castle in the cloud
I'll probably reach a conclusion that
probably my dreams are only for me …..

In a minute.

the minute passed.

i did.

if your heart needs to speak

if your heart needs to speak, let it.

it may hurt someone and help someone,
it may cause a smile and result in a tear,
it may need discretion, and it may need timing,

but if your heart needs to speak
and if it is the truth it must be told...

if your heart is confused,
then allow it time...
give it a quiet evening alone.
where it can reach through the confusion
using the words of God as its hands
separating out the chaos
throwing those Demons away
leaving the Truth.

then the Truth can be told.

there is more

there's more happiness than sadness
      reflecting in the mirror
            of what is both you and i.

there is laughter and there is love,
      there are images of a closeness
            that will never, ever die.

i won't give up on you today,
      nor will i tomorrow,
            next month, or even next year

you're a very special person
      who deserves to find that place
            where God and His love are near.

so if the courses that you choose
      dictate that in our travels
            we must go our separate ways

there's love for you in every sky,
      throughout all the night, in each new dawn,
            now, forever, and a day.

spaces beyond

spaces beyond
are calling
to me.

someday
i'll follow the
drifting clouds and
discover those places.

all
memories of me

and
of my having been

will be lost.

like a
sudden spring shower

i'll

be

gone.

The Hidden Chamber

...*Fantasy*...

...*Dreams*...

* The dreamer *

See him?
Look at him and laugh:
He's a dreamer.

He dwells in illusions
Of peace to come
And of a self-less love
And of truth
And faith
And hope.

See him?
Poor boy,
He's a fool.

He talks about
No more war,
About friendly neighbors,
About racial justice,
About a living God.

See him?
Don't cry,
He's crazy.

He thinks he can help
Stop the fighting
And end the hate
And give equality to all
And live in peace
And love.

See him?
Look at him and laugh:
He's a dreamer.

And still, Hope

and
as this
black demon
that's haunting
my heart starts his
campaign to force me to
think we'll always be apart
I turn thoughts to times when we
were happy together and our
hearts felt as tho they
were light as a fea
ther, and I see
our love is
guiding
our
futures
with a hand
that is so care
ful and kind that I
feel in the future true
happiness we'll find and we
may be together till the end of
time

the dream world

Whenever I see
two lovers kiss,

I get lost
in a dream world…

…where you and I are the two,

our lips are doing the kissing

with our bodies pressed together as one,

our hearts, and our lives, are beating the same rhythm,

I am safe, secure in your arms, and you are in mine,

the world spinning around us is tranquil and at peace

and all is as it should be ….

…A dream world…

…and I am lost.

My Simple Fantasy

My fantasy is simple

When the sun rises
    It finds you and me
             Together

As the day blossoms
    It illuminates and enhances
             Our smiles

When dusk arrives
    It finds you and me
             Together

My fantasy is simple

across the skies

Across the skies
igniting the clouds
with orange flames of passion
the sun echoed the fire in my heart
as the arms of night enfolded the sun
and your arms embraced my body.

the warmth of the sun
secure in its place in the spinning
of the cosmos
and the warmth of our hearts
secure within the fortress
of our love…

both at peace
both knowing that tomorrow
a new day of sunshine
and of love
will bring new life
and new happiness
to the earth.

opposites

We came together from opposite ends
of the universe
our time lines of different lengths

the history that had formed us had molded
two very distinct shapes
our cultures produced specific, separate value sets

your view of today rooted in your past
my view of today floating in some future

you a realist with detailed thoughts of now
me a dreamer with fantasies of tomorrow

our common bond a caring for humanity
and a God that lives today.

We came together from opposite ends
of the universe
and loved.

like a dream

It is so hard to believe.
        It was like a dream.
                I was there . . . with you.

The entire day was out of a
        paperback novel where
                suddenly everything is…perfect.

The world was inconsequential,
        anything outside the effects of your smile
                just didn't matter.

For a few hours, we were the most
        important thing in the universe.
                For a moment, we *were* the universe.

It is so hard to believe.
        It was like a dream.
                We were there…together.

how long?

How long am I satisfied
        once I have kissed your lips
        once I have held you in my arms
        and we have danced through the night?

How long does it take
        until I miss your shining eyes
        until I need your sparkling smile
        to brighten the world around me?

How much time passes
        from the time I hold your hand
        from the time we embrace in the moonlight
        to the time I begin to long for you again?

How long until my heart
        calls for your heart
        calls for your love
        needing you here to be complete?

....

the longing, the loneliness begins
                as soon as we part.
                instantaneously, immediately,
                incessantly.

drifting to you

even as he was in the
midst of his teaching, i was drifting, drifting,

drifting to a world where you and i

... embraced tightly in the parking lot
after an evening of dancing and laughter.

...shyly, carefully drifted toward each other
that night of our first kiss.

...strolled hand in hand across the grassy fields
enjoying the warmth of the august sunshine.

...sat quietly watching the tv movie,
my arms around you, your head on my chest.

...laughed with the excitement and thrill
of the white water sweeping us through the gorge…

…kissed in the walk-in closet in the master bedroom
on the second floor of the second model home we visited.

…i drift, and i dream, often,
 of those moments with you…

Some People

Some people
Need cigarettes filled
With marijuana or hashish
To make their idle dreams
More than just a wish.
But not me.

Some people
Need cans or bottles
Of alcoholic booze
To make their lives
Run easy and smooth.
But not me.

Some people
Need little tablets
Of uppers and pep pills
To make their lives bright
And destroy all their ills.
But not me.

Some people
Depend on fighting
To conquer their troubles
And to make all their worries
Float away like weightless bubbles.
But not me.

Some people
Need money and power
To complete the things they do.
But all I need,
All that I'll ever need,
Is you.

I'll take these four days

I'll take these four days
put them in a frame
to remember
the dream
that
was
.

I'll take the framed dream
put it in a steel box
hide it away
to open
again
on
lonely nights
.

all by myself I will open the box
take out the frame to remember
the happiest time and the
most wonderful woman
that God brought
to my life so
close to my
heart
.

I'll remember us: you with
your life and me with
the dream and I'll
look at what
happened
and

I'll smile.

<u>The Dungeon</u>

The Dungeon

(do not tarry here long – there is a much better life beyond!)

Avernus

Help me
I am sinking into a dark pit of desolation,
I am shrinking, decaying, beyond all consolation.
I have ruined my life, tortured my soul:
Life's not worth living - my bloods growing cold.
Please - help me die, help me escape from this place
Help keep me from harming the rest of my race.

I realize too late just what I have done.
My friends are all gone; I've lost all I'd won.
My errors in love I've tried to disguise
With masks of ideals founded on lies.
The weak I have mocked - their faults criticized
Until now I'm part of what I despised.

If I was ever a man, I'm now just a shell:
A self-centered inhuman bent on destruction in Hell.
My family is kind; my friends were the best,
But I am a failure - need I tell the rest?
I thought I was right. What an ironic twist!
Now I'm lost and confused in a veil of gray mist.

My time has run out; now I must leave
And enter the world - and make people believe
That I'm really happy and I'm really cool,
When deep down inside I know I'm a fool.
It's too late now to stop my decline:
My soul is the Devil's and no longer mine.

maybe its just me

maybe it's just me
getting used to life as it really is
boxing up my emotions again
away where they belong
and can't be seen

then going on with the world
accepting reality for what it is
donating to the past those
silly hopes with all those
 illusive fantastic dreams.

maybe it's just me
having put my fears behind me
looking for you to face tomorrow
with less sorrow and unhappiness inside

feeling I have unwittingly caused
some sadness to be borne in you
wishing I could erase those feelings
that you unsuccessfully try to hide.

maybe it's just me
reading something in the air
feeling a distance between us
I cannot comprehend or fully read

when we hug feeling the difference
but not being able to say
if it means you've decided
you know just what you really need.

maybe it's just me
thinking you are pulling away
wondering if the space will
become so wide and the distance so great

that one morning soon
you will have become so involved
in your private life again
you won't be able to fit me in at all.

Maybe it's just me.

63

once in every hundred or so years

Once in every hundred or so years
if you're standing all alone
in the right spot
in the barren desert
on the right day
during the longest, hottest week
of the endless summer,

an incredible event will occur:
the moon will suddenly cover the scorching sun,
the burning sands will instantly cool,
he world will be completely new and different

for a while.

You eclipsed my world:
the world that I had made.
you blotted out the scorching trials of daily living.
you covered the strains of stress with your smiles and your laughter,
you cooled the burning memories of the past with your living music,
you made the journey worth traveling with your hugs and your kisses,
you gave me a completely new and different and absolutely wonderful
world

for a while.

During those fantasy weeks
I was shielded from the merciless desert sun
by a perfectly fitting disc of happiness that cooled the earth's evils,
that made the armor around my heart fall useless to the ground
as I strolled carelessly from day to day with your hand in mine.
you allowed me to show you the hidden cares and desires
that had fled the burning heat of the surface years before

for a while.

But I didn't see that the world from my vantage point was
 different than the world from your vantage point and I didn't see
 that though I was shielded you still had your own suns,
                            your own journey.

I didn't see that what had become my new journey and my new world
 had not become your new journey or your new world and
 I forgot that when the time for the eclipse is over there is a
 Bright Flash and if you are looking then it can blind you with pain

for a while

for a long while.

Once, a hundred or so years ago,
 I was standing all alone in the right spot
 on a barren desert on the right day
 during the longest, hottest week of the endless summer
 and an incredible event occurred:
 you suddenly covered the scorching sun,
 the burning sand instantly cooled,
 happiness surrounded me,
 the world was completely new and different
 and it was Unbelievable!

for a while.

overheard...

I shouldn't have been there,
but I was.

I shouldn't have listened
but I couldn't avoid it
because I was in the
chair right next to
you when you
talked to him

in that way
I thought
was for
me.

I shouldn't be here.

I feel like such a fool.

if i could have been

if i could have been
what i wanted to be
to you for you
then maybe you
would have
wanted to be
with me
more than
not.

but
i
guess

i
wasn't.

you
didn't.

you
aren't.

you
can't

i'm
alone.
done.
gone
terminated.

gone

It was as though a giant hand
       descended from the sky
   and wrapped its thirsty fingers
      around my body, my life:
             and squeezed.

Suddenly, I was tired, fatigued, sleepy,
      all my vitality, my energy, my
    drive was gone, gone, gone away…
I was drained, drained of all pleasurable
      desires of normal men;
   I was hungry, thirsty, starving,
      my stomach empty, my mind void
         of rational reality.

My thoughts had no beginning, no end;
     no content, no purpose:
   there was no reason for life or death,
     for existence or non-existence:
   there wasn't even a reason for
         reason itself.

I lay there as I lie here now,
     or sat there, or stood there,
  or whatever; it didn't matter,
    it doesn't matter,
        it never will matter…..

miss

i miss you.

The Lonely Boy

Once more the dawn breaks over the eastern plains
Illuminating a life plagued with winds and rains,
And a lonely boy is crying again.

The hours fly by as time hurries on
But for him they drag: his girl is gone
So the lonely boy no longer belongs.

When noon comes 'round the sun shines bright;
Yet in that boy's life it's dark as night,
For the lonely boy has lost the fight.

Why did she leave - she said she'd wait,
But a flirting girl can share no such fate,
So she turned from him and closed the gate.

Beneath the afternoon sun the world moves slow
As he wonders where his girl did go,
Now his life is shattered as the lonely winds blow.

In the evening mist he sits alone,
His heart beats hesitantly with sorrowful tone,
And his agony cries out in an endless drone.

Tomorrow he'll arise from the place where he's lying,
And he'll act as though he'd never been crying,
But deep inside his heart, the lonely boy is dying.

how can six hours

how can six hours
be
so long a time?

why has an eternity
passed
since i beheld your smile?

why is my heart crying
for
your presence, your love?

six hours – six hours
six long lonely hours
i miss you so much!

chaos

The clouds of mistrust, dishonesty, and deceit
are crowding the sun with a mist so deep
that there's not much hope that a new dawn will occur
or that for this black plague there will ever be a cure.

Trust is a word in a long-forgotten past
where a family was more than just an empty cask;
where parents and their children believed in each other
and there was an element of peace between a man and his brother.

Once Love meant more than sex, and man's god wasn't money,
and our leaders were brave, and death wasn't funny,
there was a time when you could smile without getting in trouble,
and once youth meant more than the scum of society's rubble.

The bottom of the barrel has now reached the top
and is destroying and infecting the rest of the crop.
Lost morals have caused the dilution of our values and beliefs,
and no longer Peace or Love can anyone keep.

New Ideas are struggling to show their fresh faces
but are being strangled to death by the men in high places:
the only conceptions that manage to seep through
are the corrupted and evil that from the stifled thoughts grew.

The generations in power are afraid to let go
And let others take over and run a new show,
They're all afraid to allow us to live and let live,
they're afraid that to receive, they may have to give.

If they'd lower the barriers of sex, age and color
Low enough to permit man to love one another,
then maybe they'd understand that man's destroying himself
by not reading the new books that have been placed on the shelf.

he was a bright kid

he was a bright kid
intellectually potent and
physically overpowering;

he had brains; guts; nerve;

he believed in brotherhood,
motherhood,
patriotism and the American flag;

he hated communism
imperialism
George Wallace and racism.

But his YMCA medals,
his Boy Scout Merit Badges,
his Sertoma Citizenship awards
and his Emily C. Newman scholarship to MIT

were useless

when he was drafted
and a peasant blew his brains out
in a rice paddy.

The rain.

The morning sun reflects
off the softly falling rain
that pounds a rhythm on the roof
and spatters in the drain.
It races down the window
in streams of heaven's dew
and reminds me of the time
we watched the rain, just me and you.

Then suddenly, it's gone away
and all is bright and clear:
the birds began to sing again,
with voices filled with cheer.
But I, I anticipate the day
when it will rain again,
for memories are all I have
of love and you and the rain.

my future was gone

My future was gone in much less than an instant:
Disappointment, that Jackal,
sank canines right through my heart.
With one final snap
my Dreams were sliced into ribbons,
Crushing hope, faith, and trust in that Demon of Dark.

The Ghosts of convictions that had reigned in my life
Spurted loose from Lost chasms
the attack left behind.
They gathered as one,
then soared in a flight to the heavens -
I was left to survive in my numb, half-crazed mind.

The last spirit to exit the carcass of Dreams,
Paused for a moment, then turned to face me
with piercing, cold eyes.
Dead Dreams dared accuse me,
Dropping tears on my past
Then it too took to flight, now I'm alone here to die.

i began missing you.

i began missing you
before you left the room
before i turned around
before the sentence reached its end.

loneliness thundered in my head
the instant you said you were leaving
the moment the words touched my ears
the second the meaning became clear.

emptiness gripped my heart
as the future unfolded before me
as i understood just what would happen
as you turned to leave my life.

i began missing you
before you left the room
before i turned around
before the poem even approached the end.

No warning

Without warning,
  Winding its way through the crowd,
  Scaling the walls of the stadium,

Leering, Leaping,
  The giant gargoyle Loneliness,
  Looking for a new hapless victim:

Striking me,
  Shaking me, violently jarring
  All vestige of heat from my being;

Tearing open my chest,
  Ripping out my helpless heart,
  Waving it triumphantly in the October wind;

Leaving my body frozen to the seat,
  Invisible, empty,
  Miles away from the people next to it;

Shivering silently,
  Viewing the couples, friends,
  Parents and children cheering;

So glad they can't see me
  Devastated, dying.
  Suddenly saturated with sadness…

I remember your eyes

i remember your eyes
　　　how they glittered and shone
like two sparkling diamonds
　　　when i came home.
your lips – so warm,
　　　so soft and sweet,
when we tenderly kissed
　　　each time we'd meet.

i remember your hands
　　　as we undressed
that gentle touch,
　　　that sweet caress.
your trembling body
　　　next to mine
i'll never forget
　　　'til the end of time.

i remember .. i remember
　　　days long ago
when we loved each other
　　　and our happiness flowed.
i remember.
　　　yet i can't remember why
you left me here alone
　　　for another guy.

near death

deadly darkness descended
brutally burying my life beneath a bulky, black blanket of pain,
pounding, pushing, pressing, stifling, suffocating,
causing barriers and walls to arise within.

silence was my soul companion.
no one near enough to feel the frustration of my hapless heart,
discouraged, detached, the more I drifted
the greater the distance grew.

cold crushed the essence inside,
gripping my soul and my heart with its frigid arctic fingers,
the greedy glacier grew and grew
gnawing at the fading fire.

You found me.
ignoring walls, disregarding bulwarks and barriers,
You conquered the chaos of the years
with new beginnings of Love.

You gave my heart wings
to fly fearlessly free and opened my soul
to feel the compassion and kindness
blossoming within **You**.

the light from **Your** heart
bathed all of creation with its brilliant beauty
diving down to the dungeon's depths,
destroying the darkness.

marching melodies masquerading
as wonderful words of wisdom overflowed from **Your** lips,
serenading my solitary separate soul,
matching my heart's rhythm.

You, the eternal warmth of the western summer winds
swept through my reality,
Feeding a fire of future fantastic fantasies,
Finally defeating the fading frost.

The Chapel

The Chapel

<u>God</u>

Into the clear blue sky
I gaze.
I stare.
I search
But I cannot see God.

Into great churches
I wander.
I walk with holy men.
I talk with holy men.
Yet, I cannot feel God.

Alone in my room
I pray.
I ask.
I plead.
Still, God gives me no answer.

Into the ghettos
I walk.
I stop.
I help…
Here, at last, I have found God.

It was a beautiful day, Lord

It was a beautiful day, Lord.
From the first tender caress of dawn
To the last rose-red cloud of eve
It was beautiful.

It was good to see you today, Lord.
I could see
As your children worked and played together.
I saw you in the glory of the new spring
Lilacs and the fresh velvet grass.

Your presence was magnificent today, Lord.
I sensed your being in the handshake of an old friend,
And in the warm, lazy breeze.
I felt your touch as you guided my words
That made people laugh and smile.

I'm not confident in myself, Lord.
As I become more confident in you,
I thank you for this inspiring day
That only you could possibly create.

It was a beautiful day, Lord.
From the first tender caress of dawn
To the last rose-red cloud of the evening
It was beautiful.

slow me down, Lord

slow me down, Lord,

slow enough to remember lessons I've refused to learn.

teach me moderation, Lord,
bring out the patience within me and let me use it.

> i've got to rest, Lord,
> 'cause i can't lose another round,
> i've got to withdraw and get
> my feet back on the ground.
> logic- analysis- experience:
> i must use these tools' might
> to direct the love you've given
> Lord, that it may shine true and right.

slow me down, Lord,

show me how Faith, Love and Wisdom live hand in hand.

slow me down, Lord.

A Prayer for a Girl far away

Almighty God, she's in Your hands.
You control her fate.
You determine where she lands
In this wicked world of hate.

Protect her, Lord, from any pain
And keep her safe and sound.
Fill her life with sun, not rain,
Until true happiness she's found.

If You will do only this for me,
Then my life, too, will be bright.
For this girl, Lord, holds the only key
That opens my heart and holds back the night.

She needs You, Lord

Here I am again: yes its me again, Lord,
Asking, requesting, begging for You to step in.
There's too much hurt going on in her heart, Lord,
 She needs Your help, Your strength, Your healing to begin.

She wants to do what's right with You, the great Son,
But the message is mixed, confused, and unclear.
She's so caring: she doesn't want to hurt anyone
Especially one of us she holds so close and so dear.

Please give her the strength to face this great test
No matter what the outcome, she needs You by her side
To help her make the right choice: You know what is best
To help her settle this strife: You can be her great Guide.

Please Lord, give her Love, let those tears cease to flow.
Replace them with wisdom, and calmness, and smiles.
Please give her the knowledge of how to make this pain go
And give her Peace as she continues along life's long miles.

A Prayer

Hello, Lord. It's me again,
And, as usual, I've a favor to ask:
Since You control the destinies of men,
I'm asking of You this simple task.

There's this girl, Lord, and she's gone away
To a place far different from mine.
She's heading toward a new dawn, a new day,
And she'll be there quite a long time.

While she's there, I'd just like to know
That she's safe in Your loving hands.
That no matter where she decides to go
You'll protect her with those powerful hands.

I realize, Lord, that I'm always praying
For You to give things or do things for me.
It seems, when we talk, I'm always saying
How I'd wish You'd make things be.

Yet, it's Your world, Lord, and her future is Yours,
All that will happen is Your choice alone.
But I pray that You'll help her open the doors
To a life of Love, grown from seeds that You've sown.

Teach me Lord

Teach me to love, Lord.
Tell me how to tell her about love.
Show me the path to lead her along.
Teach me to love, Lord.

Teach me to talk, Lord.
Tell me how to speak words of love.
Show me how to convey your love.
Teach me to talk, Lord.

Teach me to act, Lord.
Tell me what to do to love her.
Show me how to do what needs to be done.
Teach me to act, Lord.

Teach me to dream, Lord.
Tell me how to tell her of the morning sun.
Show me how to settle her mind and bring her peace
Teach me to dream, Lord.

I, II, III

I.   there was love

        there was loving, caring, sharing
        and dreaming
        hurting, pain, frustration
        disillusionment, disappointment
        fact of reality
        impossible dreams turned to
        tomorrow's nightmares
        but always love.

II.   there was strength

        one strength for two
        one limited strength
        limited existence
        unlimited love
        learning, experiencing…
        crying…
        renewal of strength
        God.
        Limitless love.
        Limitless strength.

III.   there is strength

        endless.
        There is God
        endless.
        There is Love
        endless.

The Highest Turret...

On Top of the World!

you are

...
recess.
time out.
stress break.
finally Friday evening.
a joyous Easter Sunday.
a cold drink on a hot day.
a hot drink on a cold day.
a reassuring hug in sadness.
a happy hug in a joyous time.
a quiet, peaceful aspen forest.
the cease-fire in the Middle East.
a clear, sunny Saturday morning.
the calm in the midst of the storm.
the serene summit of the highest mountain.
a brief burst of sanity in a very hurried, crazy world.

and I enjoy you more, and more, and more, and more ....

touching you

touching you tingles.

just us

us.

your arms sweep up and rest gently around my neck and shoulders causing the world around to begin to fade, all loneliness and coldness vanishing within the embrace of your warm, loving hug.

gazing deep into your eyes I can see clear pools of love and trust that make all thoughts of the stresses and strains of the world dwindle to become merely a speck somewhere in the background of a world of you.

deep inside a thousand, no, a million, butterflies take flight as we hold each other, the Magic that exists between you and I now surrounding us and protecting us together safe, secure, in our kingdom where Castles and Magic and Love rule in a serene, peaceful, world.

then another fantastic physical phenomenon overtakes my mind and inundates all existence when you press your body close to mine and the love flows from my fingertips to your soft, smooth back, through your shoulders, down your chest, and back into mine.

as our lips meet, electricity leaps from mine to yours to mine to yours in seemingly endless bolts of lightening that gather within us and then explode from one to another with an energy, a force that overpowers all logic and melts our hearts, our souls, our futures into one.

us.

your kiss

the shock rocked my entire physique
my knees weakened, I could barely stand.
dizzily, I staggered back, grabbing on to something close
to help me keep from falling,
to keep a complete collapse from happening.

with the speed of light the lightening spread inside,
my muscles were rendered useless,
my willpower all but disappeared,
my logic struggled for a foothold
as sanity struggled within my mind.

inside, my blood began to boil,
waves of heat pulsed through my being,
the adrenaline rushed to my nerve centers,
and I recovered,
my intellect amazingly alert, sharp, focused, aware:

suddenly it all made sense…
my muscles rippled with a new strength,
the answers to the questions of my life flooded my mind,
a new buoyancy lifted my soul
as my heart understood the message.

then our lips separated...
your eyes opened, displaying shining orbs
that illuminated the world and kept the kiss
from ending with the touch,
as your smile breached the space between us...

i wish i knew what you're dreaming

i wish i knew what you're dreaming...
        i hope it's about us.

i have to go, again,
as i've always had to go
to do what has to be done
in the world to survive
but you know, though, that as i
enter Wall Street and
make or lose money,
conduct my business.
eat at popular coffee shops,
buy and sell and trade.
talk about the President,
discuss that horrible war over there,
when is the university football team going to win,
bet on whether or not they catch the murderer,
and
do all those things that happen in a day,

i'll be wondering what you're dreaming.

i hope it's about us.

holding hands

you brought such joy

to my life, to my heart

when you held my hand in the room . . .

in the car, again holding my hand . . .

on the street, your hand in mine. . .

seemed so simple,

didn't it?

this I know.

there are some things I know
for sure,
many things I don't know about
at all…

I don't know what the future holds for you
or for me
I don't know where you'll be a year from now
or me either
I don't know what will happen with our lives
tomorrow.

I do know, though,
how I felt the day we met
when the butterflies first flew aloft
within me.

I do know
how the time we've spent
becoming friends,
close friends,
then even closer friends
has released feelings
within me I didn't know were there
has caused reactions
within my heart, my soul, my life
that mystifies me completely
and fills me with a joy
that seems to have
no limits.

I do know that now,
even after the years have past,
the butterflies still take flight
with your every look,
with your every smile,
with your every touch.

I do know
how I feel inside
today.

and
did yesterday.

and
for a long, long time.

I know.

even though

even though it is cloudy
and
rainy outside,
though the cold winds
may
chill your skin,
this is still a good day
to celebrate,
a great day
you can triumph and win.

you have the Compassion,
the Caring,
the Love in your heart
to make every day shine
with the warmth
of a thousand suns above,
plus, you have the Power,
also, from mine.

look outside now
with a new vision: new eyes
that see past
what the surface displays:
look beyond to the Truth:
see the beautiful skies
that are there for you forever,
every day, always…

summer's song

Summer's song soon, again, will close:
Its sunny days and moon-filled nights will perish
Leaving behind only new-born seeds of Autumn
And us - with memories to forget or to cherish.

Bright colored leaves and cool breezes
Will spring forth as Autumn matures and grows.
Then it, too, will die, and we'll observe the changes
As its spawn - the Winter - brings forth the snows.

Wise men have said that all good things -
From May's young flowers to November's snows-
Must reach their destiny… their ultimate… their end…
To ebb into eternal time-past's flow.

But I - I defy those men of wisdom
Who must never have smelled of love's sweet breath,
For I believe the essence of two heart's love
Will last forever - far beyond an earthly death.

Thank You For You

Thank you
For staying with me
When all others had gone.
Thank you
For changing my tune from a funeral march
Into a happy song.

Thank you
For overlooking my faults
And my silly mistakes.
Thank you
For those cute little cards
And that wonderful birthday cake.

Thanks
For holding my hand
When I was feeling down;
Thanks
For sending those smiles
That wiped away all my frowns.

Thanks
For all the laughter, the smiles
The hugs, and the kisses;
Thanks
For all the tender love
That a lonely boy misses.

Thank you
For being
Such a wonderful girl
Thanks
For being the bright sun
That brings life to my world.

A song for you

The sun shined
> Brightly from blue skies above
> Flooding all the Earth with love...
And shined on you.

The breeze blew
> Spreading warmth over the land
> Touching all the hearts of man...
And it touched you.

The birds sang
Up above you
And cats purred
When they touched you
And the world smiled
All around you
Cause there was you.

My heart leaped
> When it first beheld your smile
> And prayed that you would stay awhile...
Just me with you.

My heart sighed
> When it knew your love was mine
> 'Til the eternal end of time...
Me loving you.

there are so many things

There are so many things we haven't done
That are wild, and crazy - but they might be fun,
There are places to go and things to do
And sights to see so fresh and new -
More people to meet we've never seen
And unreached goals and distant dreams.....

But this will take time: years and years
With moments of laughter, and maybe of tears,
But just the same I'd like you to stay
To be with me always to brighten the way:
So together those distant stars we'll reach
And together we'll sun on an eternal beach.

they probably thought i was crazy

They probably thought i was crazy
laughing
in the car by myself
when i was thinking of you
and how crazy YOU are.

I keep smiling - i can't stop! -
thinking of you -
and us together -
the fun we have -
the ever-expanding comfort zone
that envelops you and
when we're together

I just can't stop smiling!

Addi

the music began in the corner
then spread throughout the room.
it chased away frown after frown
and every trace of gloom.

gaining momentum, it then began
to spread smiles across everyone's face.
happiness in its finest grew
at an incomprehensible pace.

the glowing brightness from all the eyes,
the love electrifying the air,
emitted from that tiny corner
from someone just sitting there.

the laughter and the giggles
of that playful baby girl
had for a moment erased all their troubles
and made this a happier, brighter world.

Angels

The Lord has sent me angels
At times throughout the years,
To help me with my burdens,
To brush away my tears.

Most I did not recognize
As we traversed the miles,
Calming nods, thoughtful advice,
Soft encouraging smiles.

He knew, though, that I needed more,
He brought me to this place,
His Pure Love reflected in your eyes,
His Grace upon your face.

Then as our friendship blossomed
(Undoubtedly His Will),
You took some Angel magic
And touched it to my ear.

Suddenly the world of song
Was new and bright and fun,
Filled with Joy and Love: His Word
Proclaimed for Everyone!

Soon the time will come once more
For me to travel on,
Strengthened by an Angel now
While singing joyous songs.

You have brought more to my life
Than you will ever know.
I wish you Peace and Joy, and Love
Wherever you may go!

We will dance forever

There will always be music,
And when the music plays,
There will be us.

Dancing.

Just us,
In the afternoon.

Just the two of us.

Dancing.
In the dining room.

Our own song.

Our own world.
Our own love.

Dancing.
Always dancing together.

Just the two of us.

We will dance,
heart to heart.

We will dance forever.

until we met

Until we met

I'd never seen the flames,
never felt the warmth,
never trusted the sun,
never believed in a tomorrow
of love.

I was afraid
of sunsets and of darkness
until your love
ignited the fire in my heart
that burns within even when
the darkness surrounds me.

Now my clouds
my dreams,
my castles
are forever warmed
by the memory
of your love,

and I thank you.

.....Now its time to go back to your world.

Hopefully you have found
some old memories
and
enjoyed some new adventures
while touring this castle.

May God be with you
to give you eternal strength and love
Whenever, Wherever
you find
or build
Your castles.

(W. Michael Armbruster has also written
Hugs and Other Wonderful Stuff, 1997)

Michael Armbruster is a Colorado native who first saw his poetry and articles published in the Aurora Advocate many years ago. The poems in this collection were selected to meet the demand of those who read his first book (1997) and clamored for more. They reflect experiences, emotions, and people he met as he traveled a very winding path in life working in disparate industries such as hospitality, construction, and information systems while earning his undergraduate and Masters degrees.

Mike's simple, honest, open style appeals and is meaningful to readers from all walks of life, various educational levels and backgrounds. Teens and adults have welcomed his poetry, as he offers heartfelt thoughts, feeling, and insights that span the years.

Made in the USA
Coppell, TX
21 March 2022

75320899R00070